anythink

D1442274

Space Voyager

Neptune

by Vanessa Black

Bullfrog Books

Ideas for Parents and Teachers

Bullfrog Books let children practice reading informational text at the earliest reading levels. Repetition, familiar words, and photo labels support early readers.

Before Reading

- Discuss the cover photo. What does it tell them?

- Look at the picture glossary together. Read and discuss the words.

Read the Book

- "Walk" through the book and look at the photos. Let the child ask questions. Point out the photo labels.

- Read the book to the child, or have him or her read independently.

After Reading

- Prompt the child to think more. Ask: What are your favorite facts about Neptune?

Bullfrog Books are published by Jump!
5357 Penn Avenue South
Minneapolis, MN 55419
www.jumplibrary.com

Copyright © 2018 Jump! International copyright reserved in all countries. No part of this book may be reproduced in any form without written permission from the publisher.

Library of Congress Cataloging-in-Publication Data

Names: Black, Vanessa, 1973– author.
Title: Neptune / by Vanessa Black.
Description: Minneapolis, MN : Jump!, Inc., [2018]
Series: Space voyager
"Bullfrog Books are published by Jump!."
Audience: Ages 5–8. | Audience: K to grade 3.
Includes bibliographical references and index.
Identifiers: LCCN 2017033292 (print)
LCCN 2017029891 (ebook)
ISBN 9781624966880 (ebook)
ISBN 9781620318485 (hardcover : alk. paper)
ISBN 9781620318492 (pbk.)
Subjects: LCSH: Neptune (Planet)—Juvenile literature.
Classification: LCC QB691 (print)
LCC QB691 .B67 2017 (ebook) | DDC 523.48—dc23
LC record available at https://lccn.loc.gov/2017033292

Editor: Jenna Trnka
Book Designer: Molly Ballanger
Photo Researchers: Molly Ballanger & Jenna Trnka

Photo Credits: NASA images/Shutterstock, cover; Sveta Orlova/Shutterstock, 1 (girl); Nostalgia for Infinity/Shutterstock, 1 (drawing); glenda/Shutterstock, 3; Mark Garlick/Science Photo Library/Alamy, 4; JPL/NASA, 5, 13, 23bl; B. A. E. Inc/Alamy, 6–7; NASA/Science Source, 8–9, 23tl; Atlas Photo Bank/Science Source, 10–11; Tristan3D/Shutterstock, 12; Science Photo Library - Mark Garlick/Getty, 14–15; Vadim Sadovski/Shutterstock, 16; JPL/USGS/NASA, 17; Carlos Clarivan/Science Source, 18–19, 23br; Roger Ressmeyer with Ian Shelton/Corbis/VCG/Getty, 20–21; adventtr/iStock, 23tr; JPL-Caltech/NASA, 24.

Printed in the United States of America at Corporate Graphics in North Mankato, Minnesota.

Table of Contents

Cold and Blue

What is the eighth planet from the sun?

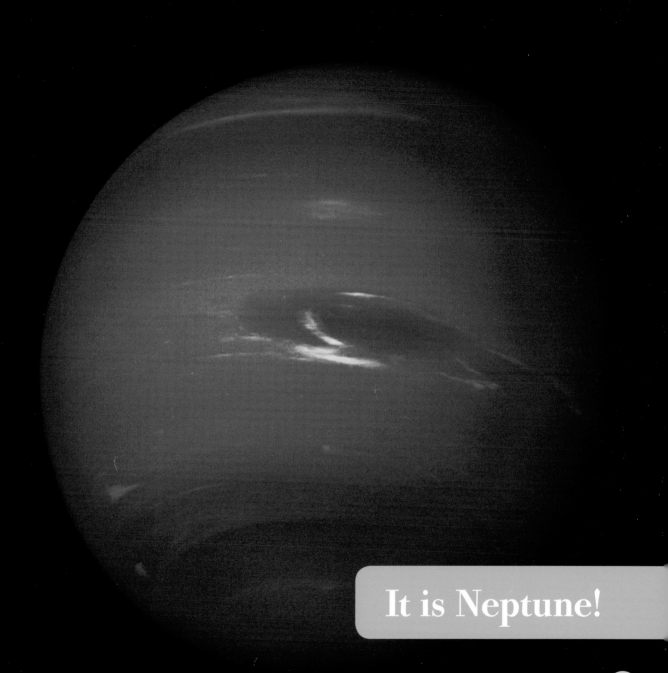

It is Neptune!

Look at our
solar system.

Neptune is far
from the sun.

It is cold.

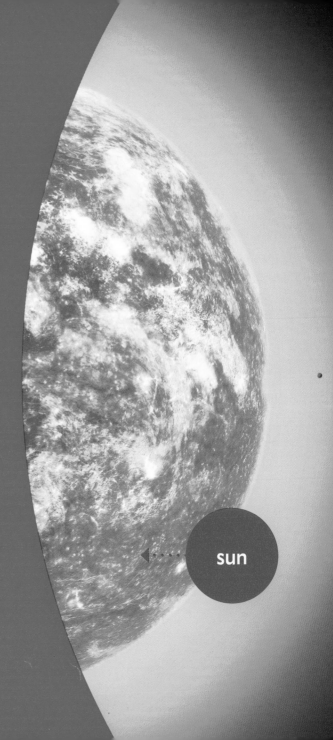

sun

Neptune

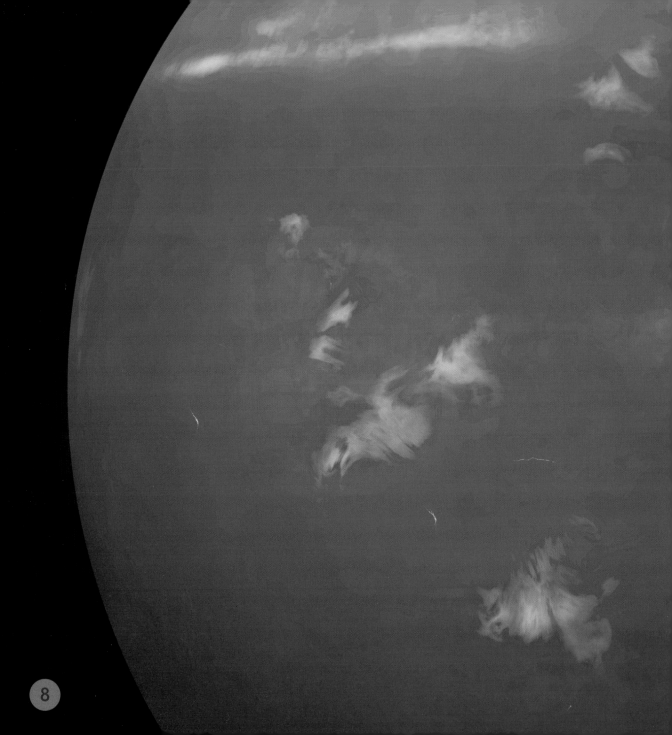

It is made of gas.

The gas is ice.

Why?

It is very cold.

The gas is methane.
It makes Neptune
look blue.

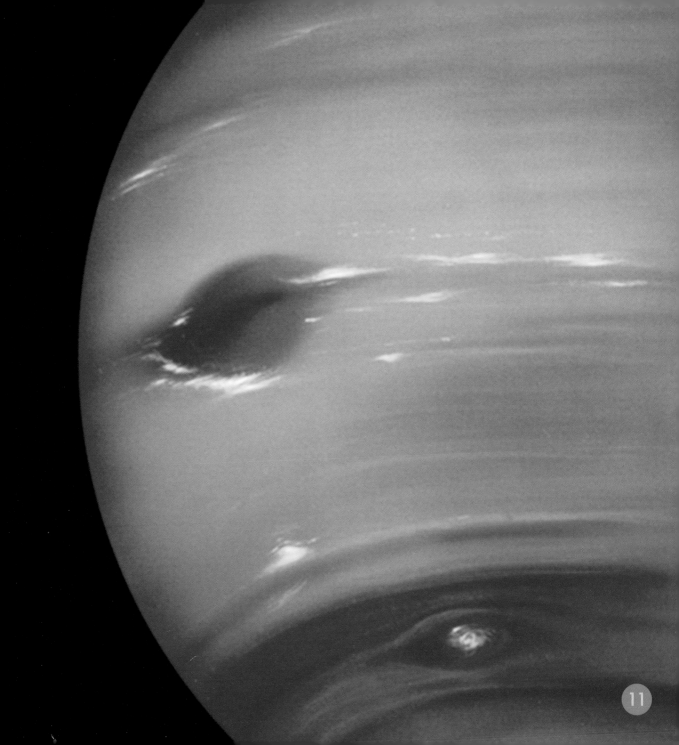

It is very windy.

There are storms.

storm

13

It has six rings.
They are thin.
They are hard to see.

rings

It has 13 moons.

Triton is the biggest.
It is colder than Neptune!

Triton

Neptune is far away.
Only one spacecraft
has gone by it.

There is more to explore!

A Look at Neptune

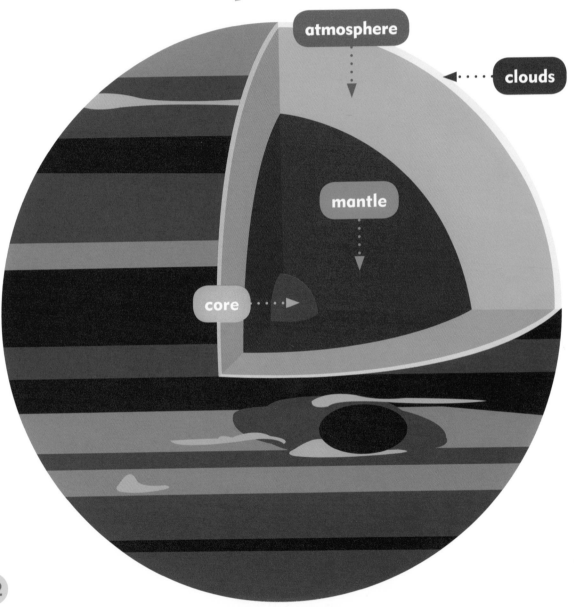

Picture Glossary

gas
A substance similar to air that expands to fill space.

solar system
The sun and other planets that revolve around it.

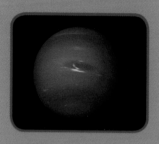

planet
A large body that orbits the sun.

spacecraft
Vehicles that travel in space.

Index

To Learn More

Learning more is as easy as 1, 2, 3.

1) Go to www.factsurfer.com

2) Enter "Neptune" into the search box.

3) Click the "Surf" button to see a list of websites.

With factsurfer.com, finding more information is just a click away.